IMAGES
of America

OAKDALE

Between 5,000 and 6,000 people came by train, horse and buggy, and automobile to the grand Rose Carnival and Parade in Oakdale in 1911. The celebration, sponsored by the Women's Improvement Club, was a huge success. The program included motorcycle races, May Pole dances, vaudeville performances, a ball game, a choral concert, and a lavish evening ball. At the time, the population of Oakdale was only a little over 1,000. (Courtesy of the Oakdale Museum and History Center.)

ON THE COVER: J.B. Stearns opened a blacksmith shop on West Railroad Avenue in Oakdale in 1886. He not only shod horses but also manufactured buggies and wagons. J.M. Harray joined him sometime later, and they employed 10 blacksmiths. They closed the buggy manufacturing part of the business in 1915, as the growing popularity of automobiles made buggies obsolete. W.B. Taylor and Sons still operate a metal fabrication business in this building today. (Courtesy of the Oakdale Museum and History Center.)

IMAGES
of America
OAKDALE

Friends of Oakdale Heritage

ARCADIA
PUBLISHING

Published by Arcadia Publishing
Charleston, South Carolina

Printed in the United States of America

Library of Congress Control Number: 2023938574

For all general information, please contact Arcadia Publishing:
Telephone 843-853-2070
Fax 843-853-0044
E-mail sales@arcadiapublishing.com

Visit us on the Internet at www.arcadiapublishing.com

This book is dedicated to the memory of Tim Haidlen, whose pioneering work in collecting reminiscences, stories, and pictures of Oakdale's early residents formed the foundation upon which this work was created.

CONTENTS

Acknowledgments

This book has been a longtime dream of Friends of Oakdale Heritage volunteers. The images, except where noted, are from the collection of the Oakdale Museum and History Center. Don Riise, Daryl Wiley, Doug Divine, David Cross, and Susan Arnett Byars worked to research, identify, and organize the images and text. Don Riise scanned hundreds of images. Barbara Torres, Suzanne Lauzon, and Diane Korupp helped with editing. David Cross also generously provided many images from his extensive private collection. We wish to thank Janet Lancaster and Laura Mesa of the McHenry Museum and Bill Maxwell of the Bank of Stockton for sharing their advice, expertise, and resources.

The board of the Friends of Oakdale Heritage has operated the Oakdale Museum and History Center in the 1869 Tom Prowse house since 2009. The commitment of board members Barbara Torres, Don Riise, Suzanne Lauzon, Diane Korupp, Gretchen Haidlen Arbini, and Cynthia Robinson has been key to preserving this important community resource. Without it, our book could not have been completed. We also wish to thank our many visitors to the museum who share their stories and their enthusiasm for Oakdale's colorful history.

INTRODUCTION

The town of Oakdale (Oak Dale for a short time) was named in honor of the beautiful oak trees that stretched for miles along the banks of the Laquisimas River. There are many reasons for the location of the town, all contributing like the roots of an oak tree. They reach back a couple of decades before the formation of the state of California in 1850. The section of California that eventually became Stanislaus County was scarcely populated at that time. Fighting between the indigenous people (Yokuts) and the Mexican armies had been continuing for several years. In the 1830s, the fighting became intense along the banks of the Laquisimas River west from Knight's Ferry and downstream to the San Joaquin River.

Prominent among the Indian tribes of this area was a man named Cucunuchi, who was given the Spanish name Estanislao, and resided at Mission San Jose for a few years. He was employed by the padres and recognized as a hard worker, an alcalde, and a vaquero. However, he became greatly disturbed by the treatment his fellow Indians received and by the influx of people displacing the tribes along the rivers to the east. He escaped from the mission and organized tribes to discourage further displacement, particularly along the Laquisimas River. He organized the stealing of horses and livestock from newcomers occupying their tribal lands. This caused fear and anger among the settlers and led to Mexican soldiers searching out these tribes to eliminate them. Although the tribes put up very successful defenses, they were eventually subdued. Chief Estanislao evaded capture but eventually surrendered at Mission San Jose. He was later granted a pardon by the Mexican governor. Ironically, Estanislao was so admired for his valor that the Laquisimas River and the newly established county were named Stanislaus in his honor.

With the end of the Indian wars, the land on both sides of the Stanislaus River began to be populated by farmers and ranchers. Those along the south bank of the river saw the opportunity to develop large plots of land with grain and livestock. They also needed to cross the river to get to the markets of Stockton, Sacramento, and San Francisco. At the same time, the discovery of gold to the north in 1848 at Sutter's Mill had a dramatic effect in California as prospectors came from the rest of the United States and Europe to the gold fields of the Sierras. These factors created opportunities to provide crossings over the rivers running from the Sierras west to the San Joaquin Valley, including the Stanislaus.

The Stanislaus River was too deep to easily cross during the seasonal Sierra runoffs, which encouraged the construction of ferries. In 1849, the Taylor Ferry was the first to be built across the Stanislaus. It was sold in 1850 and became known as the Heath and Emory Ferry, located about three and a half miles east of the future town of Oak Dale. This location provided a continuation of the original Mariposa Military Road from Stockton south to the southern mines. To the west of Oakdale, other ferries operated in the early 1850s, including Holden Ferry, Cotton Ferry, Islip Ferry (near the future site of Langworth), and the Burney Ferry (near the future site of Riverbank). These ferries were in business for several years. But entrepreneurs saw profits awaiting the one who could provide more reliable transportation across the river.

The owners of the Stockton & Copperopolis Railroad recognized the opportunity before them. They proposed to take advantage of the need for transportation to the southern mines and to the grain and livestock customers south of the Stanislaus River by creating a railroad line across the river. They had already established a line east from Stockton to Copperopolis and decided to develop a line turning south from the existing Copperopolis line at Peters. The line would then continue over the Stanislaus at Oak Dale to Visalia. To accomplish this, the Stockton and Copperopolis Railroad merged with the Visalia Railroad to become the Stockton & Visalia.

When a coalition of adjacent property owners—Z. and F.M. Cottle, A.J. Patterson, A.E. Purcel, A. Burnett, and A. Leitch—heard of the search by the Stockton & Visalia Railroad for a river crossing, they approached the company with an offer. The coalition would donate land on the north and south sides of the river in exchange for the company building a train depot on the donated land in the newly established town of Oak Dale. The company accepted the offer because the land provided the best point to prevent flooding of a railroad bridge during periods of high water, making it reliable throughout the year. With an agreement in place, the railroad developed its line from Copperopolis south across the Stanislaus River.

On November 14, 1871, an engine of the Stockton & Visalia (sold December 1871 to the Central Pacific Railroad) crossed the bridge over the Stanislaus River and continued about a mile to the depot at the center of the new town. It was reported at that time that the town consisted of 21 buildings. These buildings housed businesses serving the immediate needs of the surrounding farms and traffic to the southern mines. They included a livery stable for Harden, Schadlich & Hamlin on the east side of the railroad, J.B. Stearns's blacksmith shop, and Dr. Hazen's office and dwelling on the southeast corner of Fifth Avenue and F Street. Nearby was a barber shop and Buddington's saloon. On the west side of the tracks, Robert Sydnor had a general merchandise store and post office on the northwest corner of F Street. In the rear of that building was a Chinese washhouse. A Mrs. Dodson provided lodging at her Dew Drop Inn and a Mr. Tuohy ran the Oakdale Hotel and a general merchandise store. There was a restaurant in a building brought from nearby Langworth, a grocery store, a skating rink, and a few homes. The town was on its way to being the center for the transportation of grain and livestock to markets to the west as well as services to the gold mines. It was also attracting new residents because of its available water, excellent soil for a variety of crops, and healthful climate.

The town was laid out in a rectangular grid. In the center of the grid was the land owned by the railroad, running north to south. Running parallel to the tracks were the two main avenues: West Railroad (now Yosemite) and East Railroad (now Sierra) Avenues. Running east and west of the railroad were the lettered streets, with F Street at the center. East Railroad and West Railroad Avenues were the early business districts, which developed quickly between E and I Streets. But like most towns of this era, the buildings were made primarily of wood. After a fire destroyed a large portion of the businesses on East Railroad Avenue between F and G Streets near George Greiersen's wood-framed store, he built the first brick building in Oakdale. Several other buildings on that block were later destroyed by fires and replaced by brick buildings. West Railroad Avenue suffered likewise. From E Street to I Street, many original buildings were destroyed by fires prior to the 1900s. Some were replaced by brick buildings that lasted decades, only to be demolished in the 1960s and 1970s and lost forever. Early buildings like the Oakdale Hotel, Dieke's Hotel, the White House Hotel, and one of the earliest buildings, Moulton's Hall, burned and were never replaced. In 1888, the Independent Order of Odd Fellows established a large two-story brick building not only for their own use but also for community events. It is still in use today. Buildings north and south of F Street along West Railroad and East Railroad Avenues were changing with new services.

In 1897, a corporation formed by Thomas S. Bullock, William H. Crocker, and Prince Andre Ponistowski became the Sierra Railroad. In March of that year, grading was started from Oakdale to Jamestown and on April 24, the first mile of track was laid from Oakdale. The line to Jamestown was completed and on November 10, nearly 4,500 people traveled from Oakdale to Jamestown to celebrate the arrival of the first train. Although the completion of the Sierra Railroad was a success for freight to and from the Mother Lode, it had a devastating result for Oakdale. The town was no longer the center of transportation for freight to the southern mines and some commercial services were no longer needed. However, there was still a local need for transportation of agricultural commodities grown around Oakdale. In 1904, the Santa Fe Railroad expanded its freight services east from Riverbank to the southern border of Oakdale. This also increased the options for shipping local crops west. Local businessmen saw opportunities and began diligently expanding services. They purchased land and constructed grain warehouses and other commercial buildings to meet the needs of the growing population.

Agriculture has been a sustaining business since Oakdale's beginning and continues to be today. Agricultural products have changed over the years, but the soil has continued to support a wide range of crops. The initial crops like wheat, barley, and other grains were followed by almonds, Ladino clover, and fruits and vegetables. These same fields provided for the growth of the livestock business with large areas for grazing and an expanding number of dairy farms.

After years of discussion, the town of Oakdale was incorporated in 1906 to become a California "general law city" with a mayor and city council. The first mayor was an Oakdale pioneer and business owner, J.B Stearns. During this time, it was obvious that water was needed from the Stanislaus River to provide for the growth of agricultural interests and livestock grazing. In 1909, the Oakdale Irrigation District was formed and water was diverted by canals, flumes, and tunnels to the inland areas of Stanislaus County and to the city of Oakdale. Not only did this expand agricultural opportunities, it also created a need for new buildings and businesses for the community. That same year, the Rodden brothers built the First National Bank on the site of the first commercial building (Sydnor's) on the northeast corner of F Street and West Railroad Avenue. The building is still there today with its iconic clock tower, and continues to be Oakdale's landmark.

The early 1910s saw further commercial developments, particularly along Third Avenue between E and G Streets. There was also a major change in transportation. Many businesses changed from providing services by and for horses and carriages to the sale and maintenance of automobiles and trucks.

The images that follow begin to tell the story of many of the people and events that influenced the growth and quality of life in Oakdale, a city with an evolving history. There is more to tell, more to explore, and more to learn. We invite you to come to Oakdale and enjoy a walk along our historic streets. Stop by the Oakdale Museum and History Center. Enjoy what it has to offer and step back in time.

One

EARLY DAYS

Cucunuchi was one of the Lasquisimas tribe, a subgroup of the Yokut people living in the Central Valley of California. He was named Estanislao when baptized by a Spanish priest at Mission San Jose. In 1828, he led a confederation of Yokuts in rebellion against Mexican generals Vallejo and Martinez. This larger-than-life sculpture by Oakdale artist Betty Saletta honors Cucunuchi, the Yokuts, and other native people of California. (Photograph by Don Riise.)

The Lakisamni tribe of the Yokut people occupied the Central Valley for millennia. They placed woven tule mats over pole structures to create semi-permanent lodges. Their diet included fish, game, and acorns, which were all plentiful along the banks of what would later be named the Stanislaus River in honor of Estanislao. This image is from Lewis H. Morgan's 1881 work *Houses and House Life of American Aborigines.*

This flat-bottomed ferry is typical of the kind that crossed the Stanislaus River in the early days. The ferryman's job could be hazardous, especially during the winter and spring when unpredictable flows and floods could sweep them and their boats away. Even when the river was behaving, frightened horses, mules, and livestock could be troublesome.

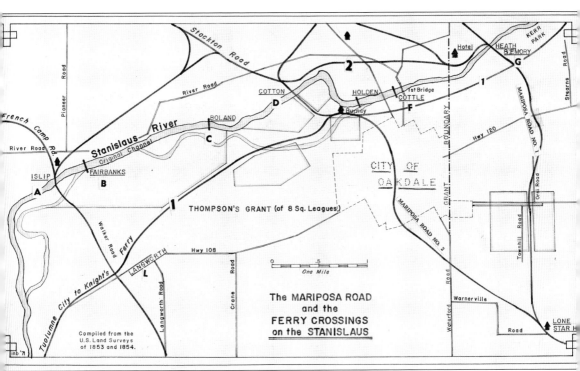

The MARIPOSA ROAD and the FERRY CROSSINGS on the STANISLAUS

Compiled from the U.S. Land Surveys of 1853 and 1854.

Soon after the discovery of gold in California in 1849, several ferries were established on the Stanislaus River near what would become the town of Oakdale. Some of the flat-bottomed ferry boats were nine feet by thirty feet and large enough to carry wagons and teams of horses or mules and cattle. The heavy traffic between Stockton and the southern mines paid the ferrymen well, but they had expenses as well. Besides the cost of their boats, they paid a $36 per year license fee and were required to post a $5,000 bond. Zora Cottle and his nephew Francis Marion Cottle were cattlemen who owned at least 500 acres along the river where they established a ferry, as can be seen on this map. At the time the earliest ferries were established near what became Oakdale, the area was still part of Tuolumne County, and the river was the border with San Joaquin County. (Courtesy of the *Oakdale Leader*.)

The Armstrong Ranch was typical of those in the area before the railroad bridge crossed the Stanislaus River and a post office was established in Oakdale. Ranchers might dry farm hundreds of acres of wheat while also raising beef or dairy cattle, sheep, and hogs. Dennis and Elizabeth Armstrong raised 11 children on their ranch, shown in this drawing from the late 19th century. (Courtesy of Jacque Armstrong.)

Since the 1850s, the rolling hills near Oakdale have provided grazing land for tens of thousands of beef cattle. By the 1870s, the railroad provided opportunities for expanding markets and made it unnecessary to drive cattle long distances overland. Here, cowboys on the Gatzman ranch in 1904 are ready to gather and brand young calves. From left to right are Al Gatzman, Chuck Gatzman, George Stapleton, and Hiram Duncan.

Before the availability of water for irrigation, dry farming was the norm. Thousands of acres of wheat were planted in the area around Oakdale. Teams of 12 to 20 horses or mules pulled the large combined reapers and threshers. Here, a crew harvests Sam Capp's crop on the Claribel Ranch.

Harvesting crews traveled from farm to farm to bale hay in the grueling heat of the 1890s, when this picture was taken near Oakdale. Hay was a much-needed commodity to fuel the horse and mule-powered transportation of the time. While gasoline and steam power were available, both posed a serious fire threat in dry grain and hay fields.

In 1871, the Stockton & Visalia Railroad announced the construction of a trestle across the Stanislaus River at a spot where the banks were high and narrow. Robert Sydnor, postmaster in nearby Langworth, quickly purchased land near the proposed railroad line and built a store. He convinced the government to move the post office to the area called Oak Dale for its ancient and abundant live oaks. Soon, business people and their families from Langworth, Knights Ferry, Stockton, and places much further afield moved to the new town to take advantage of the commercial opportunities created by the railroad. The name was later changed to Oakdale.

The Elevated Drive-way.

These two bridges put the ferrymen out of business in the Oakdale area. The railroad bridge in the background was built in 1871, and a bridge on this site in the foreground was constructed soon after. Locals called it the "wagon bridge," and during harvest, dozens of wagons drawn by mules and horses crowded along it bringing grain to the train depot and grain warehouses in town.

After grain was harvested on farms around Oakdale, it was transported to town to be milled into flour by the Stanislaus Milling Company or to fill warehouses owned by Haslacher & Kahn, A.L. Gilbert, and others. Brokers ultimately shipped to national markets via the railroad. Old-timers recalled seeing wagons and mules backed up for more than a mile waiting to unload.

This Southern Pacific engine is positioned on the circular turntable in Oakdale, just past the depot. It allowed steam engines, which could only go short distances in reverse, to turn around and return in the direction from which they had come. In 1898, the local newspaper expressed fear that the "flying switches" the Stockton train was making on the turntable would eventually result in injuries. (Courtesy of the Bank of Stockton.)

The Sierra Railway Company's steam locomotive engine No. 3 was often in Oakdale. The company was formed to connect the Central Valley to the southern Mother Lode. Transportation of passengers and freight began in 1897 with the completion of the line from Oakdale to Jamestown. Engine No. 3 enjoyed a second career in film classics such as *High Noon* and *Back to the Future* and television's *Petticoat Junction*. (Courtesy of the Bank of Stockton.)

SOUTHERN PACIFIC DEPOT, OAKDALE, CAL.

E.C. Crawford, the longtime station agent and telegraph operator for the Southern Pacific Railroad, came to Oakdale in 1875. He is easily identified by his uniform in these photographs both outside and inside the depot. Throughout his long life he was active in civic affairs, and was the unsuccessful Prohibition candidate for Stanislaus County sheriff in 1886. As a volunteer firefighter, Crawford was injured in one of the many fires the town experienced in its early days. He returned to his post at the Southern Pacific station after 10 weeks. In 1908, he was elected city trustee. The *Oakdale Leader* reported that "he was as near perfect a man as a human being could be . . . his life was replete with good deeds, secret charities, and generous activities."

One of the first commercial buildings in Oakdale was the store constructed in 1871 by A.W. Moulton and S.G. Valpey on the southwest corner of West Railroad Avenue and G Street. Both men had previously had businesses in Knights Ferry. They did a thriving business in Oakdale and were soon able to enlarge their store. While Mouton established himself in Oakdale, Valpey remained in Knights Ferry.

A.W. Moulton sold general merchandise, engaged in real estate development, and was the local agent for Wells Fargo & Company in the 1870s. After adding a second story to his building, he renamed it Moulton Hall and it served as the post office, the Wells Fargo office, a general merchandise store, and a venue for balls, public meetings, and musical performances. It burned down in 1890.

Benjamin Sisson and his team pull a large load past the Kornmayer Hotel in this photograph taken about 1882. Joseph Kornmayer built the hotel in 1878. It was destroyed in 1887 in a huge fire, which also burned two saloons, two barbershops, and Reeder's Chop House (where the fire started). While inspecting the damage, Kornmayer fell into a deep open well and died of his injuries.

Benjamin Sisson (at right holding the toddler) was a New York native who moved to the area in 1870 after a chance meeting with Henry Langworthy on an ocean-going steamship. Sisson quickly established a successful drayage business and was known as a "man of strict integrity and honor . . . possessing a cheerful disposition." He and his wife, Ida, 21 years younger, raised eight children in Oakdale.

Rutherford & Adie,
Proprietors

Oakdale, Cal.

Commercial

Lodging House
and Saloon

Robert Rutherford and C.P. Adie, both early California pioneers, owned the Commercial Lodging House and Saloon, one of Oakdale's oldest, dating to at least 1875. The saloon and a clothing store operated on the first floor and the hotel or "lodging house" was on the second floor. Located on East Railroad Avenue, it burned in 1886 and the partners replaced it with a brick structure in 1887. In the early view of East Railroad Avenue below looking east over the train depot, the Commercial Lodging House and Saloon can be seen along with the Hoffman Café, a garage, and a blacksmith shop.

A PART OF OAKDALE. OAKDALE, ~CAL. -4130-

Saloons and hotels catering to railroad passengers were soon established near the new train depot. Hubbel's Sample Room stood on West Railroad Avenue between F and G Streets. It was one of several saloons doing a thriving business in early Oakdale. John Hubbel is pictured here in 1883. This building, like many other early buildings, burned. Hubbel replaced it with a brick building in 1885. It still stands on what is now Yosemite Avenue. He served seasonal hot or cold mixed alcoholic drinks and sold smoking tobacco and cigars. In 1886, he paid F. Fisher $8.75 for labor on an iron roof in an effort to reduce the fire threat. Fisher's own shop on East Railroad Avenue was destroyed by fire in 1888.

Anna and William Dieke stand in front of their hotel in the photograph above. The Oakdale Hotel was one of several located near the train depot. They advertised the "best accommodations in town with the best quality liquors." Regular meals were offered, but if guests went hunting in nearby grain fields, the Diekes would cook the game to order. Their kitchen was famous in the Central Valley, and the hotel was the frequent venue for private parties and large public suppers. Dinner after the Masquerade Ball of 1898, for instance, could be had for 75¢ per couple. But it was not all hard work. The Diekes often visited their relatives in San Francisco. In the photograph below, their daughter Mamie is at the wheel in this souvenir from the famous Cliff House.

The White House Hotel, like the Oakdale Hotel, advertised reasonable rates and the best accommodations in town. Rebuilt in 1884 after a fire destroyed it, the building was on the northwest corner of H Street and West Railroad Avenue next to the *Stanislaus Wheat Grower*, Oakdale's first newspaper. A popular coffee parlor was added in 1886. In the above photograph from 1887, William and Mary Woods, owners of the hotel, are on the balcony at left (under the windmill) with their dog. Below, their grandchildren and friends are seen in a donkey cart in front of the hotel. The donkey gives the camera a plaintive look as seven girls squeeze into the cart and four little boys pile onto its back.

The building above was constructed by Robert Lovell in 1884 of locally made bricks on the northeast corner of G Street and East Railroad Avenue. It housed a saloon and jewelry store as well as Lovell's harness shop. The building still stands and is now a restaurant. The baby pig in the foreground obligingly cleans the streets before there was an organized effort to rid the streets of horse manure and other litter. In the early days, hogs, which could grow to hundreds of pounds, were allowed to roam free and were identified by their owners' individual ear notches. The *Oakdale Leader* complained in 1892, "For a long time the town has suffered from the depredations of privileged swine." The photograph below is of East Railroad Avenue showing the area just north of the Lovell Building.

E.C. Reeder backs his team up to the dock at the Southern Pacific depot. He is picking up a load of beer to distribute to some of Oakdale's many saloons. It is no surprise that Reeder came down firmly on the side of those opposing a local ordinance to prohibit the licensing of alcohol sales. The divisive issue was first proposed soon after the town was incorporated in 1906.

Blacksmithing was a much-needed service in early Oakdale. Here, Albert Corrigan (seated) is pictured in his shop. Corrigan, born in Oakdale in 1880, opened his own business when just 21. He also served as the town constable for 43 years and once arrested the locally notorious "Rattlesnake Jack" O'Rourke. In his obituary, the *Oakdale Leader* described him as "a man no one could find fault with."

George and Sadie Morrison are shown here at the time of their marriage in 1894. Morrison, who had operated a butcher shop, was sworn in as Oakdale marshal in April 1907. In 1909, while attempting to stop two men near the train depot, he was shot in the chest, abdomen, and wrist and hit his head on a train rail when he fell. He was carried to Dr. Thompson's sanitarium where it was determined that he could not be moved but needed more extensive treatment than the local doctors could provide. Dr. Stillman from San Francisco was summoned to operate. The businessmen in town raised $515 "inside an hour," according to reports, to pay the surgeon's fee. Morrison recovered and returned to his job, but sadly died in 1915, reportedly of a brain tumor.

E.C. Wood came to Oakdale to operate a saloon on West Railroad Avenue. He added to his income with the "one-armed bandits" on the counter and sold real estate and fast horses. When the town went dry, Wood (known as "Pussyfoot") was appointed town marshal and then city tax collector and Oakdale's first chief of police. He served for 21 years. (Courtesy of the Bank of Stockton.)

E.C. Wood is pictured here with his wife, Lizzie Capps Wood, and their nephew Maurice "F.C." Hartsoc, whom they raised. After retirement, E.C. was elected city trustee and served as acting mayor for a time. Lizzie was described as a woman of "strong character and fine personality." Maurice was a math whiz who attended Stanford University and obtained a law degree.

$50 REWARD !

STOLEN

From pasture near Oakdale, One Dark Sorrel Horse, Branded **W** on Left Hip, brand upside down; weight about 1100 pounds; six years old; had on one-half old shoe; stiff in forelegs; walks as if he had been foundered.

I will pay $25 for return of horse, and $25 for arrest and conviction of thief.

M. V. BYRUM.

Address all information to R. B. Purvis,
May 29, 1889.   Sheriff of Stanislaus County.

Though his horse was not in top shape, M.V. Byrum was willing to pay for its return and for the conviction of the thief who stole it. This notice was sent to the sheriffs of neighboring counties. Byrum was an early entrepreneur using Oakdale as a base while engaging in ranching, farming, and mining. He could afford to pay for the return of his foundered, stiff-legged horse. (Courtesy of David Cross.)

The old Oakdale jail on East Railroad Avenue was a small 15-by-15-foot building used primarily to hold prisoners until they could be taken to the county jail in Modesto. By 1917, it was judged "entirely inadequate in size and sanitary conditions," yet continued to be used for at least 20 more years. Though it was constructed of iron and brick, Walter Rickey reportedly sawed his way out in 1922.

Two

GETTING DOWN TO BUSINESS

Bennie Sisson (left) and E.L. Barkis are pictured here. In 1894, Barkis advertised in the *Oakdale Leader* that he would "buy anything you have to sell and sell anything you want to buy." The enterprising businessman came to Oakdale in 1889, and besides his retail business, he was involved in ranching and mining and advertised his services as a notary public.

Oakdale's first newspaper was the *Stanislaus Wheat Grower*, which began in 1881. Two years later, it was purchased and became the *Oakdale Graphic* and was published until 1917. The *Oakdale Leader* began publication on January 3, 1890, and eventually out-competed the *Graphic*. The *Leader*, published weekly, has continued to chronicle life in Oakdale for over 130 years.

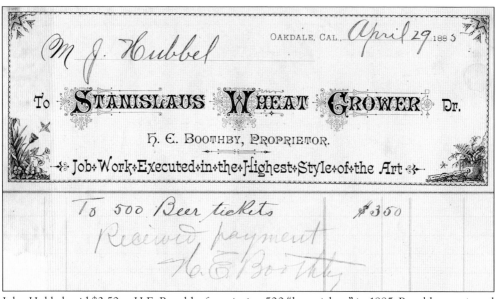

John Hubbel paid $3.50 to H.E. Boothby for printing 500 "beer tickets" in 1885. Boothby continued to use the *Stanislaus Wheat Grower* name for his printing business even after the newspaper by that name had been taken over by the *Oakdale Graphic*. Boothby and the publisher of the *Graphic* were bitter political enemies, and Boothby eventually bought the *Leader* with E.L. Shipman in 1897.

Well aware of the fires that plagued early Oakdale, George Greiersen built his general merchandise store of brick and advertised it as the "largest fire-proof brick store" in the county. Besides offering the latest in ladies' fashions from San Francisco and farm equipment such as plows and mowers, Greiersen served as an agent for "four first-class fire insurance companies."

Frank Lewis was the proprietor of City Livery, on the northeast corner of Fourth Avenue and F Street and owned by Lewis and several partners. He offered "first-class rigs and gentle horses" for rent as well as a large corral and plenty of stable room for transient teams. He had some competition from the Yosemite Livery and the Nevada Livery, owned by M.A. Lewis.

Farmer's Home Saloon was a popular spot over the years. Along with beer, which was ice cold in summer thanks to its state-of-the-art "Siberian refrigerator" and "comforting and strengthening" Kentucky whiskey in winter, the saloon offered a reading room with newspapers and the latest magazines and books. It burned in 1899 but quickly reopened. (Courtesy of the Bank of Stockton.)

The proprietor of Farmer's Home Saloon accepts a delivery from the Stanislaus Soda Works in this photograph from about 1895. Opened in 1890, it was always a busy place on East Railroad Avenue. It closed in 1913 when the town voted to go dry in a series of very close elections. Amid charges of voter fraud, the "drys" won the day in January by three votes, 376 to 373.

The Rodden Brothers store advertised as "the oldest established general merchandise store in Stanislaus County, selling first-class goods at lower prices than any other store in the county." In 1889, this store on West Railroad Avenue narrowly escaped being burned. In 1895, the brothers closed the store to concentrate on their banking and real estate ventures. Their sister Lizzie Rodden is second from right.

Oakdale's Independent Order of Odd Fellows was organized in 1875 with the mission to "improve and elevate the character of mankind." In 1888, the members moved into their new building, shown here when it was nearing completion. It still stands on what is now Yosemite Avenue and continues to serve as a meeting place and commercial space.

A SPECIAL INVITATION

Is extended to all to call and see the

GRAND OPENING DISPLAY

—OF—

SPRING MILLINERY GOODS

—ON—

Tuesday and Wednesday, April 8th and 9th, 1884.

—THE—

PARISIAN PATTERN BONNETS

AND NOVELTIES

AT MRS. P. L. HUNTLEY'S MILLINERY STORE,

WEST SIDE OF RAILROAD AVENUE,

OAKDALE.

While her husband, P.L. Huntley, was building homes, churches, and commercial buildings in town, the enterprising and talented Clara Huntley, shown below with her husband and children, was busy with her popular millinery shop. The *Oakdale Graphic* reported that "crowds of ladies called to inspect the new store . . . [which] was decorated in elegant taste." She made frequent buying trips to San Francisco and offered the latest styles at reasonable prices. She was regularly listed among the business people of the town in the 1880s. A few other women were also on the list. They were primarily teachers, seamstresses, or operators of lodging houses. When her shop burned in 1888, Clara Huntley quickly moved to the White House Hotel and resumed business.

Jacob Haslacher and Louis Kahn established the Bank of Oakdale in the two-story building in the center of this picture in 1888. The bank failed in May 1905 as a "result of excessive loans to the Haslacher and Kahn Company," according to the *San Francisco Chronicle*. Louis Kahn died on May 28, 1905, at age 50 of a self-inflicted gunshot wound that was deemed accidental.

In 1894, C.C. Wood was the first dentist to establish a permanent practice in Oakdale. Prior to that, dentists would come into town and set up temporary shops in one of the hotels and advertise for business. Another option for patients was to travel to San Francisco or Stockton. Wood is pictured here in his office on the second floor of the Bank of Oakdale. (Courtesy of the McHenry Museum.)

Brothers Ed (left) and Henry Shadlich were entrepreneurial young men. Here they are in their first business, a cigar store. The Shadlichs went on to distribute Union Ice and to be extensively involved in ranching, dairy farming, and real estate development. They were major stockholders in the Oakdale Creamery, where Ed was manager and was key to expanding the market for Oakdale butter to San Francisco and the Bay Area.

Before the days of residential refrigerators, ice was delivered door to door to fill home ice boxes. In 1899, Shadlich Brothers became the local distributor for the Union Ice Company, California's largest provider of ice. It shipped ice to local distributors via the railroad. Shadlich Brothers also delivered wood and coal when there was less seasonal demand for ice.

The Arctic Ice House was owned by Charles Offer, a native of Hungary. He had purchased Greiersen's general merchandise business and added cold storage and home delivery of ice and wood to his list of services. In 1897, he advertised that his entire stock would be sold for cash and "sacrificed in order to close up quick as other business requires my immediate attention." He moved to Stockton.

The Hop Lee Laundry occupied one of the oldest buildings in Oakdale. It was the town's post office before becoming a laundry in the 1890s. It continued as a laundry until its last owner, Tong Low, retired in 1962. Two notable public servants, March Fong Eu and Harry Low, were born in this building. Fong Eu said, "We were the original two Chinese American politicians in California and both from Oakdale."

H.F. Meyer established City Market in Oakdale in about 1889 on East Railroad Avenue. He later sold the business to his brother A.E.H. Meyer, who moved across the tracks to West Railroad Avenue. Meyer occasionally also sold venison and bear meat as well as beef, pork, and mutton. His building was destroyed by fire in 1913 but he rebuilt, and his son William operated the business until 1964.

A.E.H. Meyer welcomes customers in his butcher shop about 1900. According to the *Oakdale Graphic*, the German native "came to Oakdale with little capital, and with sagacity and pluck has steadily advanced." He "was the best judge of beef on the hoof in the state of California," became a volunteer firefighter, and was active in politics. He expanded his business and sent meat to neighboring communities by wagon and by rail.

The Stanislaus Milling and Power Company was established in 1894 by David Tulloch and his son Charles, a graduate of the State University at Berkeley, later the University of California. The two had operated a mill for many years in Knight's Ferry under the name Tulloch & Son. In 1899, they moved the milling operation to Oakdale where it was run by power generated by their Knights Ferry plant. The mill produced high-quality flour from the area's abundant wheat crops. Local residents had the "pleasure of eating the 'staff of life' made from the flour of their own wheat," according to the *Oakdale Leader*. The milling company was sold in 1904 to A.B. Haslacher of Oakdale and the Frankenheimer brothers of Stockton when Charles Tulloch decided to concentrate on the electric power business. This building still exists as part of the A.L. Gilbert complex. (Courtesy of David Cross.)

Capital $300,000 Stock.

300,000 SHARES

LOCATION OF WORKS, STANISLAUS COUNTY, CAL.

Incorporated under the laws of the Territory of Arizona

NUMBER

219

SHARES.

X-RAY OIL AND DEVELOPMENT CO.

Oakdale, Cal. January 13th 1902

This Certifies that Sarah E. Ames is entitled to

Fifty Shares of the Capital Stock of

X-RAY OIL AND DEVELOPMENT CO.

Transferable on the books of the Company by endorsement hereon and surrender of this Certificate.

SECRETARY.

INCORPORATED MARCH 1901

PRESIDENT.

Shares $1.00 Each.

In 1901, local entrepreneurs backed by Stockton and San Francisco venture capitalists advertised the opportunity to buy cheap the stock in the new X-ray Oil and Development Company. They were assured of "oceans of oil" under the ground just waiting to be discovered and that Oakdale had "better ground for oil gushers than Texas has, judging from surface indicators." The company bought 640 acres of land north of town in what was known as the Robinson tract and started to drill. The *Oakdale Graphic* urged its readers to "buy X-Ray oil stock and support a home enterprise." George McCabe, an Oakdale merchant, was president of the company. By early 1902, they had gone down 850 feet and run out of money.

A.T. Wood operated this store and invested in commercial real estate. In 1902, the horse pulling his delivery wagon was spooked by a passing team of mules and ran out of control on West Railroad Avenue. It frightened other horses hitched along the street and ultimately badly damaged Wood's wagon, but there were no serious injuries to man or beast. (Courtesy of the Bank of Stockton.)

A lone businessman heads toward the train depot in this view of the corner of West Railroad Avenue and F Street. In 1904, Louis Baer moved his dry goods store into the corner building and C.U. Byington's newsstand and stationery shop was next to the Odd Fellows Hall. Both moved again by 1909, when the Rodden brothers built their iconic First National Bank on this corner.

Before refrigeration was widely available, drying was the most affordable method of preserving and shipping fruit. Prior to 1870, most dried fruit came from Europe. Oakdale's climate proved perfect for growing and drying peaches, plums (prunes), and apricots. Proximity to the railroad meant that access to huge markets in the East could be had with reasonable shipping costs. Drying yards like this one were common in the area. (Courtesy of David Cross.)

The Pacific Pea Packing Company was established in 1906 by entrepreneurs from Wisconsin and Kansas. Peas were planted in the fertile soil south of Oakdale and special equipment for harvesting and canning arrived that year via the Southern Pacific Railroad. The first crop was canned in 1907. This photograph was taken in 1909. From left to right are Ben Yeager, Sam Kaufman, Ingells Kellas, John Kellas, Ed Shipman, Ben Williamson, and Frank Hobson.

The A.L. Gilbert Company was established in Oakdale in 1892 as a lumber business when Gilbert was just 21. In 1900, he opened a grain brokerage business and later built a warehouse and milling operation. He was instrumental in the incorporation of Oakdale in 1906 and in the formation of the Oakdale Irrigation District. Seated next to the scale, he oversees weighing sacks of grain.

In 1922, John Tryon of Angels Camp joined A.L Gilbert to form the Gilbert-Tryon Company. They sold grain and hay, poultry and livestock feed, fertilizer, and seed, as well as insurance. Pictured here with their first truck are (from left to right) Ben Medina, Henry Wren, Ed Hasbrock, Fred Gilbert, John Tryon, A.L. Gilbert, and Lawrence Gilbert. The partnership dissolved in 1936.

Peter Jorgensen manufactured a variety of carbonated drinks. His special flavors included orange and lemon soda, root beer, and sarsaparilla. He delivered to residential and commercial customers. The *Oakdale Leader* commended him on annually painting his buildings and fences on the corner of First Avenue and I Street and proclaimed that "his strict attention to business, upright course, and universal courtesy has won him the confidence of his fellow citizens."

Business was good for Peter Jorgensen's Oakdale Soda Works. In 1907, he purchased this truck to make deliveries more efficient. He manufactured a variety of sodas but also sold brands such as Bromo-Kola, which was "guaranteed to cure headaches." The *Oakdale Leader* reported that "the pure food and drink laws have no terror for Jorgensen" as "he would not sell anything he would not drink himself."

W.J. Hughes opened a small grocery store in 1889. Within a few years, he was joined by his brother and together they greatly expanded the business to include a wide range of general merchandise. In 1904, the brothers moved into their own newly constructed building on the corner of West Railroad and E Street. The second story, advertised as the Hughes Opera House, was the site of dances, traveling performances, and basketball games. (Courtesy of the Bank of Stockton.)

O.Z. Bailey's team was a familiar sight on the streets of the town, as he moved everything from hay to large equipment to buildings, making good on his promise to "move anything that is loose on both ends." Here he makes his way south on West Railroad Avenue with a team of 12 mules. The head mule looks skeptically at the fellow cleaning in front of the Live Oak Inn.

Many of Oakdale's prominent merchants and businessmen gathered for a group photograph about 1908. "Judge" W.A. Griffin, the editor of the *Oakdale Leader* and ever the Southern gentleman, is in the second row, fourth from right. Merchants like Billy Hughes (first row, second from right) complained of trash accumulating on West Railroad Avenue, prompting the city to begin regular trash pickup.

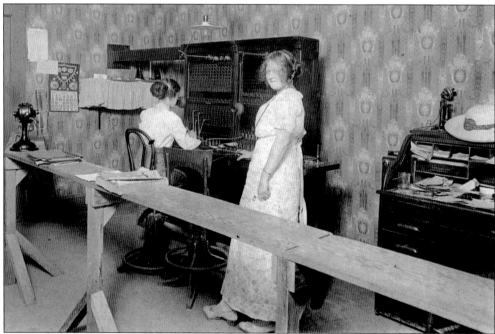

The Sunset Telephone Company secured 20 subscribers in 1895 to their new telephone exchange in Oakdale. The charge for service, which included local calls, was $1.50 per month. The *Oakdale Graphic* insisted that "lovers' talks and businessmen's orders are all alike locked in the breast of the little woman who rings the bell" at the switchboard. By 1908, Essie Capps (seated) was manager of the office, assisted by Belle Ralls.

Oakdale's iconic First National Bank was built in 1909 by brothers Edward and William Rodden. Edward was the bank president, and William was the cashier. The building boasted a vault of steel embedded in concrete with walls 21 inches thick. In the 1909 *Report of the First National Bank*, the value of the "banking house, furniture & fixtures" was $12,345.68. Its advertising motto was, "A Good Bank in a Good Town." The bank identified itself as a "home institution, organized and entirely owned by Oakdale people, with the interests of Oakdale and the Oakdale Irrigation District held above all else."

William Rodden, head cashier, awaits customers in the new First National Bank building. Rodden was rumored to have kept a Colt .45 close to hand under the window. Personal service was a hallmark of the local bank, which encouraged customers to open accounts even with small deposits. They promised to furnish a passbook, checks, and most importantly, necessary instruction. In 1909, the bank offered four percent interest on savings accounts.

Working at the desk behind the scenes in the new bank building is Alban Rydberg (seated.) He started as an assistant teller and worked his way up to vice president. The bank annually published a list of its assets and liabilities in the *Oakdale Leader* for all to see. The public was assured that while the bank was managed along conservative principles, it stood ready to invest in the community.

The First National Bank was organized in December 1904 with "a paid-up capital of $60,000." In 1909, it moved into the new building on the northwest corner of West Railroad Avenue and F Street. The first board of directors included (from left to right) Paul Brichetto, J.C. Laughlin, Arthur Leitch, Edward Rodden, William Rodden, Ishmael Monroe, and Tom Snedigar.

In the early 20th century, some banks were allowed to issue federal bank notes with their own names printed on the note. A total of $100,000 was originally issued by The First National Bank of Oakdale in denominations of $5, $10, and $20. The local bank's charter number is 7502, and the notes were signed by William Rodden, president of the First National Bank of Oakdale, along with US Treasury officials.

Built by the Rodden brothers on the northwest corner of F Street and Third Avenue, the Bank of America building looks strikingly similar to the Roddens' First National Bank just a block to the east. The Oakdale Café also occupied a Rodden-owned building. Manuel and Gus Galas moved the Oakdale Café to this building in July 1934. The *Oakdale Leader* reported that nearly 2,000 men, women, and children attended the grand opening and marveled at the café's modern air conditioning system. They also consumed free sandwiches, ice cream, and more than 2,000 cups of Valley Brew beer. In the midst of the Great Depression, the Galas brothers were applauded for using local labor to create the "latest word in modern restaurants," their willingness to invest, and their obvious confidence in Oakdale's future. (Courtesy of David Cross.)

The job of postmaster was a coveted political appointment in the early days. Robert Benson was appointed Oakdale's postmaster in 1906 by Pres. Theodore Roosevelt. Benson was a grain farmer and deputy tax assessor and was active in local politics. He had 10 children and hired daughter Lottie, pictured here, to work in the post office. The *Oakdale Leader* described her as "the splendid clerk at the general delivery window."

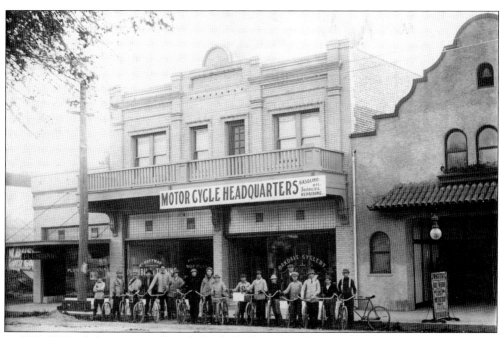

In 1911, Walter Johnson moved his Oakdale Cyclery from West Railroad Avenue to this spacious location on the east side of Third Avenue. He advertised "first class motorcycle and bicycle repair," as well as sales of new and used bikes. An H.P. Indian motorcycle with Prest-lite and speedometer could be had for $125. (Courtesy of the Bank of Stockton.)

This is one of the tanks of the privately owned Oakdale Water Works. It was established in the early 1870s to provide water to the railroad as well as to commercial and residential customers. In the 1890s, residential customers paid $1.50 per month for water delivered to their homes. By 1908, customers were complaining of rusty pipes and inconsistent supply.

Early in 1912, the city announced the first sewer system was complete. New pipes, a municipal reservoir, and a pumping station would soon follow to provide homes and businesses with a clean and reliable water supply. Concrete filled this huge wooden form to create the tank for the town's water. Constructed on a promontory south of the river, a municipal tank and a pumping station still occupy the site.

The Wright Act of 1887 allowed farming areas in California to form and bond local irrigation districts to construct necessary tunnels, canals, and flumes to divert and distribute water. The Oakdale Irrigation District was formed in 1909, after a grand rally and a local election formally approved a request to Stanislaus County to obtain water from the Stanislaus River. This early flume carrying water to Oakdale was near Knights Ferry. The availability of irrigation water heralded a shift in agricultural production away from large grain-growing operations to the development of smaller-scale intensive cultivation of fruits, vegetables, and nuts as well as permanent pasture for livestock.

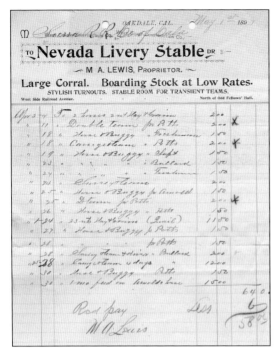

The Sierra Railroad was a good customer of Moses Lewis's Nevada Livery Stable on West Railroad Avenue just north of Odd Fellows Hall. Moses "M.A." Lewis was born in the mining town of Columbia, California, and moved to Oakdale with his parents in 1871. He boarded horses by the day, week, or month and cared for sick animals. He also offered horses and buggies for rent, charging $1.50 a day.

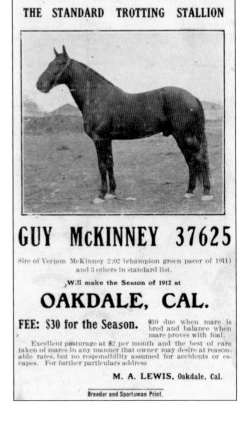

Horse racing was wildly popular in early-20th-century America. In 1912, M.A. Lewis offered the services of his Standardbred stallion Guy McKinney for $30. Guy's successful offspring Vernon McKinney won races in California and the East. He sold for the princely sum of $6,000. The McKinney bloodline produced many winners over the following decades. Guy McKinney stood at stud at J.B. Stearns's ranch along with Stearns's two stallions.

Southern Pacific's engine No. 25, a gasoline railcar, is pictured here at the Oakdale depot. The development of these futuristic-looking gasoline-powered cars was an attempt to provide more affordable passenger transportation on smaller lines. They were manufactured from 1905 to 1917, and though considered to be ahead of their time, they were also plagued by mechanical difficulties and eventually were removed from service.

In 1913, The Nightingale and Sivley store moved into a new building constructed by A.T. Wood on F Street. The store is seen here on the left looking east from Second Avenue. Alton Sivley boasted that in the few days before Christmas, "We sold $500 worth of talking machines alone." F Street was finally paved to the city limits in 1916.

A chuck wagon is replaced by an automobile bringing lunch to a harvesting crew on the Merrihew Ranch in this photograph from about 1910. Gasoline and diesel-powered machinery would soon put all these men, horses, and mules out of their jobs. Clarence Merrihew, one member of the large Merrihew clan, saw the writing on the wall and went into business selling tractors and other mechanized farm equipment.

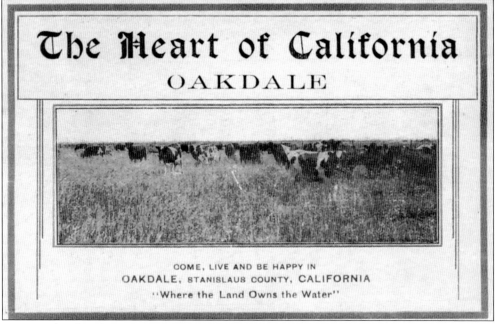

In 1915, the chamber of commerce produced this booklet touting Oakdale as "the Heart of California" and urging newcomers to "come, live, and be happy." Over the years, chamber and city officials have also promoted the town as the "City of Almonds," "the Gateway to Yosemite and Sonora Pass," "the Ladino Clover Center of America," "the West at its Best," and "the Cowboy Capital of the World."

Three

TOWN AND GOWN

J.B. Stearns is pictured here with his daughter Eva. He came to Oakdale in 1886 and opened a blacksmithing and buggy-manufacturing business on West Railroad Avenue, where he trained apprentices and employed 10 men. When the town was incorporated in 1906, he became the first mayor. His blacksmith building served as the mayor's office throughout his tenure. Stearns was a serious horseman who owned and bred racehorses as well as fine carriage horses.

Floradora was an internationally popular British musical comedy in the late 19th century. In 1899, Oakdale's own version was performed by, from left to right, (first row) Mamie Dieke, Essie Elias, and Martha Dieke; (second row) Eddie Kelly, Alton Sivley, and Joe Kahn. Kahn was a recent Oakdale Union High School graduate attending Stanford University known especially in town for his wit and musical talent.

The charming and talented Lulu Wann is shown at far right in this photograph taken in 1907 at the residence of E.N. Crow. Her popular Mandolin and Guitar Club offered recitals and performances at a number of local venues. In 1908, the *Oakdale Graphic* lamented her departure from the community when she was accepted into the deaconess training program in San Francisco.

In the photograph to the right, Oakdale Band members are pictured in 1909. Public subscriptions paid for their uniforms. Urging support for the band, the *Oakdale Graphic* stated, "A good band is the mark of good taste, superior mentality, and genuine civilization." Wright Boddy (left) and Will Tremayne are up front. Boddy became Oakdale's postmaster a few years later. Below, the band is on West Railroad Avenue in front of the Odd Fellows Hall promoting one of their many local performances in 1910. A much-requested tune was the local favorite "A Hot Time in the Old Town Tonight."

In 1910, the volunteer firemen's carnival was great fun. The festivities began with a circus parade from E to H Streets on West Railroad Avenue and then back again on East Railroad Avenue. Many of the town's most prominent citizens took part wearing hilarious costumes. The *Oakdale Leader* declared, to "describe . . . any of the participants is beyond the pen of man or woman."

These men are dressed up and ready for the volunteer firemen's parade and carnival. After the parade, circus, and carnival, a masquerade ball was held in Hughes Hall at the corner of West Railroad Avenue and E Street. At midnight, a banquet was served and prizes were awarded for the best costumes. The recently elected Oakdale Irrigation District Board of Directors won first prize for the best group.

These Oakdale Band members are in costume in 1910 to promote their appearance at the annual Firemen's Ball. They were great regional favorites, and wearing their more traditional uniforms, they frequently entertained the people of Oakdale as well as Modesto, Stockton, Escalon, and Merced. From left to right are Marion Cottle, Wright Boddy, Henry Schadlich, Ben Yeager, Ralph Jordan, Jim Griffith, Bert Warrington, Jim Titchenal, unidentified, Elmer Clark, and Alton Sivley.

Children gawk at band members and others dressed in costumes for the firemen's parade and carnival. One man dressed as a woman holds up a sign lamenting, "Oh! If Otto Durr was only single." Durr was the owner of the *Oakdale Leader* at the time.

The Rose Carnival and Parade attracted women in their finest millinery in April 1911. Organized by the Women's Improvement Club, the event was a huge success. The club was a force to be reckoned with as it lobbied successfully for a park near the railroad depot and for another property that became Dorada Park, promoted the effort to obtain a Carnegie library, and prompted many other city improvements.

Grace McKenzie sits elegantly atop a decorated wagon in the 1911 Rose Carnival Parade. She was elected Rose Carnival Queen by a wide margin. McKenzie worked in the local post office. According to the *Oakdale Leader*, she was "a popular member of the social ranks," with many friends. It was significant that she was "an east side girl," as there was always a bit of competition between the east and west sides of town.

Oakdale has always loved a parade. The Firemen's Ball parade had been a raucous affair in 1910, and the Women's Improvement Club was determined to change it up with the 1911 Rose Carnival Parade. Following grand marshal Jay Rydberg, the officers of the club rode in a beautifully decorated automobile. Other members, dressed in white, carried flower-covered arches on foot or on horseback. Moses Lewis's daughter drove her father's famous stud, Guy McKinney, for the appreciative crowd to see. Autos and horses decorated with even more flowers followed along with the band, which was dressed more conservatively than the previous year. The hit of the parade was Gilbert Baker's decorated car overflowing with children and named "Oakdale's Future." The Women's Improvement Club made a lot of money to support good causes, and the *Modesto Morning Herald* called the crowd "the largest ever assembled in the county."

Oakdale's peripatetic Presbyterian church was first built on South Fifth Avenue in 1892 before being moved to the southwest corner of F Street and Second Avenue. In 1911, it was moved again to the southwest corner of First Avenue and G Street, and a large Sunday school room was added. Many buildings were moved around town like this and sometimes repurposed. The Rodden brothers purchased the old wood-frame elementary school when the brick schoolhouse was built and moved it to Third Avenue, using it as a rooming house for a time before it was bought by someone else and moved again. Homes and other frame buildings like the church were moved from Langworth or from the countryside into town. This church building was demolished in 1960.

The Union Church, constructed in 1882 with funds raised by the women of the town, was home to at least six denominations. It was on the corner of F and Church Streets, and was eventually incorporated into the Stone Church, which is now home to the congregation of Community Christian Reformed Church.

In the early 1880s, the congregation of St. Matthias Episcopal Mission met regularly in the Union Church. This building, constructed inside and out with natural redwood and pine, was completed in January 1905 and seated about 80 people. It was consecrated as St. Matthias Episcopal Church and stood on the southeast corner of F Street and First Avenue. It was replaced by the current church building in 1957.

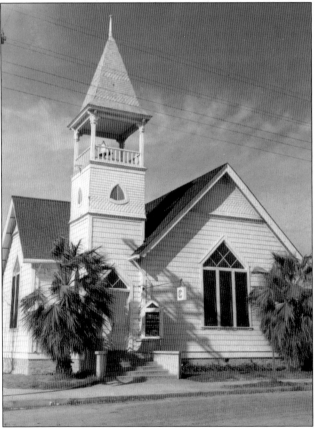

Above, P.L. Huntley (far right) and his crew construct the bell tower for United Brethren in Christ's church building. Huntley was a member of the church but also built the Free Methodist Church, the Presbyterian church, and possibly others in Oakdale. This was the sixth church to be built in town. Constructed on Second Avenue and E Street, it could comfortably seat 250 people. The pews were crowded in May 1893 for the first service. The property also included a parsonage for the pastor, Rev. W.P. Tibbet. The church building was moved and is now a private home on First Avenue and Walnut Street.

St. Mary's Catholic Church was built in 1886 on the corner of West Railroad Avenue and C Street. The newspaper reported that the Catholics believed there was "abundant missionary work to be done in Oakdale." In 1916, it was remodeled to reflect the Mission style popular at the time. It was damaged by fire in 1951, and the decision was made to sell the lot and rebuild on Oak Avenue.

The Methodist Episcopal Church on F Street was dedicated in July 1917 after a two-year construction process. Mason A.J. Steepe donated his labor to add granite waste chippings to the exterior of the building. The congregation had purchased the old Union Church for $1,000, and part of it is included in this building that could reportedly accommodate 1,000 people. It was later named Community Methodist Church. (Courtesy of David Cross.)

Oakdale's first secondary school was constructed in 1890 on the corner of Kimball and Eucalyptus Avenues on land donated by entrepreneurs Haslacher and Khan. Dubbed the Stanislaus Seminary and Normal School, tuition was $40 per year for seminary students, while normal school students attended free. In 1892, the trustees transferred ownership to the newly formed Oakdale Union High School District. The building was destroyed by fire in 1901.

During their graduation ceremony, Oakdale's high school class of 1895 was advised to "make yourself indispensable to someone" by Dr. Jewell, chancellor of Pacific University. Alonzo "A.T." Wood (third row, far left) worked as a janitor while attending high school. Afterward, he became a successful businessman in Oakdale and an unofficial historian of the town. He died at age 97 in 1970.

The site of the new high school, completed in 1907, was controversial. W.A. Patterson donated the land in an area recently surveyed as the "western suburb" of Oakdale. The *Oakdale Graphic* suggested that the move to the new site was a scheme by land speculators to increase their profits on new development. Though it looks quite different, the high school occupies the same block on G Street today. (Courtesy of David Cross.)

The 1912 Oakdale Union High School boys basketball team was known as the "Invincibles," and they proved it that year by winning the championship. They played home games in the second story of Hughes Hall on the corner of West Railroad Avenue and E Street. Standing from left to right are Polly Watson, Bert McNamera, Leslie Wilkinson, Kenneth Kaufman, and Howard Wilkinson; Leroy Kaufman is seated.

The Oakdale Union High School girls' basketball team of 1909 stands in front of the school. According to the *Oakdale Graphic*, the team not only beat Modesto, but also "walloped" their Turlock opponents that year with a score of 29 to 13, guaranteeing they would be town favorites. From left to right are Edna Stearns, Elena Crow, Florabel McKenzie, Civilla Beasley, Lelia Wilkinson, Mellie Rodden, and two unidentified.

The Oakdale Union High School baseball team of 1907 is pictured here. Their opponents from Stockton, Sonora, and other towns arrived on the train with their supporters. The total high school enrollment that year was 28 students, so it appears that a significant number of them were on the team. While fans were usually "gentlemanly," according to the *Oakdale Graphic*, Constable Corrigan's presence was sometimes required at games.

The first Oakdale Grammar School was built in 1882 on the north side of F Street between First and Second Avenues. Originally a one-story structure, a second story and rear wing were added in 1885. When the brick school was under construction, this building was pushed to the back and the children continued their studies in it until they could move into the new building on the front of the lot. Mrs. M.E. Sawyer had her hands full in November 1886, about the time the photograph below was taken in front of the school. More than 50 students attended her primary and grammar class that month. There was no requirement for attendance, and many students did not attend on a regular basis, especially if their parents needed them to help at home.

The redbrick Oakdale Grammar School was built in 1901 at a cost of $26,000 on the site of the original grammar school. Prior to construction, trustees asked legal voters to cast a ballot for brick or wood. Brick won the day. "Legal voters" were men at least 21 years old. Women would not have the right to vote in California elections until 1911 and in national elections until 1920. (Courtesy of David Cross.)

Oakdale Grammar School teachers stand in the front yard of the school on F Street in about 1910. The Presbyterian church can be seen across the street. Eva Belle Stearns, daughter of Oakdale's first mayor, taught fifth grade and is pictured at far right. By this time, teachers were paid from $90 to $125 per month and class sizes varied from 21 to 33 students.

This street scene looks north on West Railroad Avenue toward F Street and shows a major commercial area of town about 1910. By this time, brick buildings had replaced many of the old fire-prone wood structures, and a few motorcars can be seen on the street along with a horse or two.

The members of the Women's Improvement Club were not happy in 1915 when city trustees rejected the offer of a $7,000 grant from Andrew Carnegie to build a library in Oakdale. The women refused to take no for an answer, and within two years, they had secured the grant and raised $470 to purchase three lots on F and Davitt Streets. The building was completed in early 1917.

Irving Sisson (holding the rope) and friends swim in the Stanislaus River, probably without suits, as was the custom for boys in the countryside in 1895. This was a favorite spot on the north bank of the river looking east, with the first highway bridge in the background. Now gone, the bridge replaced a ferry that connected the Old Stockton Road.

Oakdale got a lot of attention with the construction of its elliptical "artificial swimming tank." Built in 1913 at a cost of $1,400, it was 60 feet by 40 feet and ranged in depth from seven inches to seven feet. It was featured in national publications such as *Popular Mechanics* and *Country Gentleman*, which recognized the innovative engineering that allowed the pool, when emptied every few days, to flush the town's sewer system. (Courtesy of Ken Terpstra.)

In 1913, the *Oakdale Leader* boasted that the town had the only free municipal swimming pool in the state and welcomed rich or poor, city or country dweller to "take the plunge." Soon, however, a 10¢ fee was charged during certain hours, and bathers were required to wear suits and supply their own. That would be no problem for members of the prominent Rodden family, pictured here with friends.

This was the home of William and Dora Rodden, which was completed in 1905 on West Railroad Avenue and E Street. His brother built a nearly identical home just a block away on West Railroad and D Street. The *Oakdale Graphic* described the residence as a beautiful "ornament to the town."

The people of Oakdale woke to two inches of snow covering the ground on New Year's Day 1916. It was more snow than had been recorded since the train depot was established in 1871. Snowball battles were quickly organized and sleds were improvised, but the snow was mostly gone by the end of the day. Snowfall in the mountains was exceptionally heavy that year, creating ongoing problems for railroad traffic. It was not uncommon for train cars coming into town from the east to be covered in snow. These pictures were taken at the intersection of West Railroad Avenue and F Street, looking west.

Four

GOING FORWARD

The Los Angeles–Camp Curry (Yosemite) Economy Run was an annual event organized by California automobile dealers and billed as the "most important motor event of the year." In 1919, it marked the formal opening of the Big Oak Flat Road. Oakdale merchants took full advantage, promoting Oakdale as the perfect launching point for the last leg of the trip, which would take more than five hours in good weather.

In 1916, Standard Oil Company purchased land for a service station in a prime location on the northeast corner of F Street and West Railroad Avenue. In the 1930s, this oversized attendant greeted motorists. Real-life attendants also wore white shirts and black bow ties. They pumped gas, routinely washed windshields, and checked customers' oil. Gasoline cost about 20¢ per gallon. (Courtesy of David Cross.)

When this photograph was taken, automobiles were replacing horses, buggies, and wagons on the still unpaved streets of Oakdale. In 1905, the state first required motor vehicles to be registered, with owners providing their own plates. In 1915, state-issued porcelain plates with five digits were displayed on the rear of the vehicle, but the proud owner of this auto displayed his on the front too.

This view of West Railroad Avenue illustrates the rapid changes taking place in town. Gone are the horses, buggies, mule teams, and hitching posts, replaced by city trash cans, cars, and businesses catering to automobiles and their maintenance. The Live Oak Inn, originally the Hotel Stanislaus, had changed its name in 1910 when the Shadlich brothers became managing partners in the business.

Elmer Endicott (left) is pictured in his drugstore on West Railroad Avenue with an unidentified man and Milton Seeber (right). Endicott's father, a physician, established the business around 1890. In 1895, Endicott was advertising his services as an undertaker and embalmer. By the time of this picture in 1921, the drugstore was highly successful, and he was active in civic affairs as a city trustee.

In 1920, Earl Anderson and P.C. Walther opened a gas and service station on the south side of F Street on the corner of First Avenue. They advertised "expert auto repairing," with Ford automobiles as their specialty. Then as now, Oakdale was a stopping point for many motorists on the Big Oak Flat route to Yosemite.

Clyde Reynolds opened his Clyde's Place restaurant on the corner of F Street and Sixth Avenue in 1932. At the time, he offered a lunch special for 25¢ and a special Sunday "raviola" dinner for 50¢. In 1936, he added six modern tourist cabins next door. He is pictured on the left with his wife, Mary, and grandson George Chappell. (Courtesy of Lynn Chappell.)

John Rocha loads milk cans onto his first truck in 1924. He transported milk from dairies to creameries in the area. After emptying the cans, the creamery personnel would thoroughly wash, sterilize, and dry the cans at the plant before Rocha returned them to the farms for the next day. (Courtesy of Rocha's Valley Enterprises.)

During the 1930s, transporting livestock by rail or driving them cross country to and from pasture began to change. Moving cattle, sheep, and pigs by truck gained favor. The Rocha family was one of the early livestock haulers to serve the Oakdale area. They purchased their first cattle truck in 1935.

By 1921, Oakdale's elementary school was overcrowded. An addition was made to the "red brick school" and the new East Side Elementary pictured here was constructed in the popular mission style on East F Street. Within a year, the enrollment was 189, and the average class size was 36. The school closed in 1966 when it was deemed an earthquake hazard. It was replaced by a hotel in the 1980s.

In 1935, Marion Corrigan, a recent University of California, Berkeley graduate, was hired to teach music in the high school and in both grammar schools for a salary of $1,760. Much loved by students, he directed the marching band, the orchestra, and the dance band. He also taught academic subjects. He is pictured here (top row, third from right) with the grammar school band in 1936. Corrigan taught for more than 30 years in Oakdale.

The above photograph shows a new building that was added to the Oakdale Joint Union High School campus in March 1923 for a cost of $80,000. Some of the furniture was constructed by students in their manual training classes, saving the district more than $3,000. The students celebrated the opening with a performance of the operetta *Miss Cherry Blossom*. The auditorium was filled to capacity and many were turned away. The photograph below shows the façade that is familiar today. It was completed in 1956 when there were 1,200 students. They came not just from Oakdale but from Knights Ferry, Valley Home, Waterford, and Riverbank.

Oakdale Union School, also known in later years as West Side and Magnolia, was built in 1939. John Hachman's bid of $198,000 was accepted by the school board to build 18 classrooms, five other rooms, and an auditorium, all in the Art Deco style. The result was hailed as one of the finest schools in the state, getting extensive press coverage and visits from admiring engineers, architects, and educators.

This charming mural, depicting a scene from Disney's *Snow White and the Seven Dwarves*, was painted in the kindergarten room at Oakdale Union School by Herman Struck in 1939. Like many artists during the Depression era, Struck was employed by the federal Works Progress Administration. Rumor had it that he had been a Disney illustrator, but the company denied having any record of his employment. (Courtesy of Janet Fogarty Medina.)

When Elizabeth Vertrees (left) married Henry Helt in 1931, she gave up her teaching job since the district had a policy of not employing young married women. That changed during World War II. Elizabeth returned to the classroom and spent 20 years teaching home economics at "Westside." The curriculum covered cooking, sewing, and home life education, which focused on "good conduct, self-discipline, poise and selection of becoming clothes."

While the girls studied home economics, the boys were busy in shop class. Using math skills and basic tools, they turned out many highly prized birdhouses, step stools, and small benches in this spacious room with its beautiful tall windows and natural light. (Courtesy of Janet Fogarty Medina.)

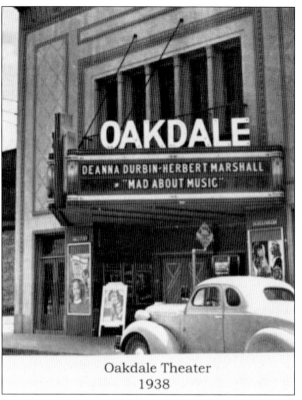

Oakdale Theater
1938

From at least 1915, Oakdale had a succession of movie houses showing the best of the "talkies" according to the *Oakdale Leader.* In 1921, the Realto opened on F Street, featuring a "monster pipe organ." In 1926, it was redecorated under new management and renamed the Oakdale Theater. Ticket prices ranged from 15¢ to 50¢. The building was demolished in 1968, and a Bank of America branch occupies the site today.

Thanks to the efforts of the Oakdale Women's Club, the Oakdale Plunge opened in Dorada Park in 1926. In 1927, about 300 people attended the special season-opening program. Local stores recognized a marketing opportunity and advertised all-wool bathing suits for $1.98 and $2.98. Though its outside appearance has changed along with the pool itself, the Plunge continues to be a popular spot in the same location.

Oakdale Calif.

The Clover City

The Dorada Clubhouse was built in the park in 1916 for $2,000, which had been raised by the Women's Improvement Club. For nearly half a century, it was a venue for dances, dramatic performances, and public gatherings of all kinds. The clubhouse burned in 1959 during the Oakdale Joint Union High School graduation party. The cause was determined to be faulty wiring. Fortunately, no one was injured.

After incorporation in 1906, Mayor J.B. Stearns had his office in his blacksmith shop. In 1908, the city rented space for a city hall from Jacob Haslacher for $5 per month. Finally, in 1920, after several years of discussion, the city bought a building on the northwest corner of G Street and West Railroad Avenue for $4,500 and spent another $5,000 to remodel it into the city hall.

Clay Dorroh (left) was born in Angels Camp in 1888 and came to Oakdale as a clerk for the Wells Fargo Express Company in 1917. He was appointed Oakdale police chief in 1945, after serving as a patrolman. He had a staff of two other full-time officers. The population of the city was close to 3,000 that year. By 1952, when the photograph below was taken, the police force had expanded to include, from left to right, Sam Riley, Dick Lepley, Dorroh, Bill Echoles, and Bob Vorhees. Until 1952, if a resident called the police between 5:00 p.m. and 8:00 a.m., an answering service activated a flashing red light at the corner of F Street and Yosemite Avenue. Seeing it, the officer on duty would call back. If he did not see the light or respond to the answering service, the resident had to call the sheriff's office to ask him to radio Oakdale's patrol car. In 1952, a system was installed that rang into the fire department, and the fireman on duty would radio the officer.

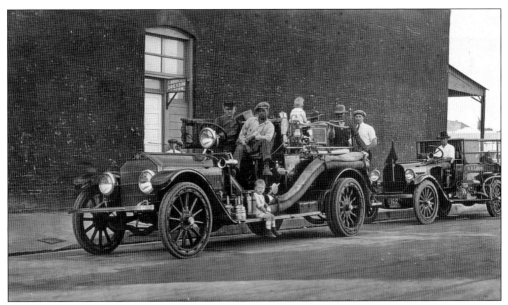

In 1923, P.E. Van Pelt was selling Dodge motor vehicles in Oakdale when he built his first fire truck, pictured here, for the Oakdale Fire Department. Within 25 years, Van Pelt Incorporated was the largest manufacturer of fire apparatus on the West Coast. From left to right on the fire truck are Conrad Hubbel, Roy Raycraft, Bobby Hubbel (on running board), a child with his back to the camera, Earl Arnett (mostly hidden), fire chief O.Z. Bailey, and Craig Davidson. Jack Brunning is on the smaller truck at right. (Courtesy of the McHenry Museum.)

By 1931, when this picture was taken, P.E. Van Pelt was already gaining a reputation for versatile high-quality firefighting equipment. He was a visionary engineer and savvy businessman who knew his market. This demonstrator model traveled around the state so local officials could get a close-up look at his quality machinery. The women are unidentified. (Courtesy of Lynn Chappell.)

Grain fires posed a serious threat in the rural areas around Oakdale. Volunteer fire chief O.Z. Bailey proposed the idea of a rural fire truck service early in the 1920s. In 1923, details of Oakdale's rural fire unit were published in *Pacific Rural Press* and *Sunset Magazine* as a model. According to the *Oakdale Leader*, area farmers had the lowest insurance rates in the state because of the efficiency of the rural fire unit and the Van Pelt Company's equipment. Support for the unit was not universal, however, as some town residents resented the cost and insisted that rural residents bear the financial burden. P.E. Van Pelt had plenty of orders from all over California as word spread about the quality, reliability, and efficiency of his equipment. At left, an operator tests a powerful pump using Stanislaus River water. Lovers Leap is in the background.

In 1932, the Almond Blossom Festival started with a parade across the new Stanislaus River Bridge, which had been recently built for a cost of $80,000. California governor James Rolph Jr. (right) was on hand to give the dedication speech attended by thousands. The program included a concert by the Oakdale High School Band and featured a dance pageant portraying the history of the area. Phyllis Nicholson was crowned Almond Blossom Queen.

In the 1920s, more than 4,000 acres in the Oakdale area were planted with almonds. So many people were motoring to view the blossoms that in 1927, the Farm Bureau decided to host a festival to promote agriculture in the area. The festival continued to be a popular annual event until it ended during World War II. Dorothy Coppetti (center) was the 1934 queen. (Courtesy of the Coppetti and Walther families.)

Anna Eastman models for photographer Roy Flood in front of a house on F Street. The elegant young woman was an accomplished dancer who turned down the opportunity to dance professionally when a talent scout saw her perform at the Almond Blossom Festival. Roy Flood and his wife, Bess, came to Oakdale in 1931 and operated Flood Studio for more than 30 years. (Courtesy of Sonya Schali.)

The Nazarene Church was constructed using timbers from the original highway bridge across the Stanislaus River that was replaced in 1932. Church members, many of whom were out of work because of the Depression, provided all the labor to build the church, which could seat 700 people. The *Oakdale Leader* applauded their efforts, saying, "The church people . . . fought their way out of the depression by building a home of their own."

Louis Meyer, owner and publisher of the *Oakdale Leader* for over 30 years, invited the community to admire his new building on South Third Avenue in January 1937. It was claimed to be fireproof, with beautiful modern tile work. It housed all the operations of the paper. The California Press Association congratulated Meyer on serving his community and devoting his efforts to publishing news "fit to print."

Stan Wakefield and Pete Cortelyou bought half interest in the *Oakdale Leader* in 1945. Wakefield, who served as publisher and editor for 30 years, is on the right wearing his trademark fedora. The man at the press is unidentified. In 1960, when Wakefield was elected president of the California Newspaper Publishers Association, Richard Nixon gave the keynote address to the organization and presented Wakefield with the gavel.

In the 1930s and 1940s, passengers lined up to board the Greyhound bus at Ira M. Delong's Stage Depot on Yosemite Avenue. DeLong sold ice cream, candy, tobacco products, and magazines as well as bus tickets. Greyhound boasted that it could transport passengers 10 or 10,000 miles. Oakdale's taxi, looking a little worse for wear, is parked at left, ready to serve arriving bus passengers.

This large Purity grocery store was built in just 45 days in 1940 for a cost of about $7,500. It boasted air conditioning and promised "strictly modern merchandising methods." It occupied the corner of F Street and Second Avenue and was considered the first supermarket in town. Bread was advertised for 9¢ a loaf, and bacon was 15¢ a pound.

Earl Haslam (left) was just out of high school when he opened the Highway Garage on the northeast corner of F Street and West Railroad Avenue in late 1915. Following World War I, he was joined by his brother William. They sold and repaired Chevrolet automobiles and operated a Shell gas station. They soon took over the livery stable next door, and expanded again in 1939 when they constructed this building.

During World War II, PG&E pledged to provide power to support "our battalions of farmers producing food by the shipload for our armed forces." W.E. Arnett (left) supervised this PG&E crew that helped to keep farms, ranches, and the cannery powered for the war effort in Oakdale. Arnett had been wounded in France during World War I and had two sons serving overseas.

From left to right, brothers Pfc. Charles H. Willey, Army Infantry flight officer Donald C. Willey, and Pfc. Almer B. Willey (Army Medical Corps) were Oakdale High School graduates who joined the military during World War II. They were on leave and visiting their parents in 1943 when this photograph was taken. In August 1944, Grover and Eulalie Willey received a telegram telling them their son Charles had been wounded in the invasion of France. The extent of his injuries were not reported. He recovered and returned to service only to be wounded again in Germany. He was awarded two Purple Hearts. In 1945, Wanda Reed and Eulalie traveled to Oklahoma for Donald's graduation from flight school. Wanda and Donald were married the next day. Charles and Donald returned to Oakdale after the war. In 1954, Donald purchased L.N. Isaac's Auto Repair on the corner of F and School Streets and operated it for decades. Donald's three sons—Daryl, Robert, and Dean—worked at the shop on school breaks. In 1981, Dean became the owner and renamed it Willey's Body Shop.

Women pick peaches in this 1944 photograph. Women took to the orchards, fields, and the cannery in Oakdale during World War II to do their part. California's fruits and vegetables fed US troops all over the world during the conflict. California's Food for Victory program announced that it was imperative that every available person help with the local harvest. Leola Kaufman, of Oakdale's Pacific Pea Packing Company, was in charge of mobilization for "C Day" to recruit workers to handle the peach harvest in Oakdale. Oakdale women were called upon to serve in a number of ways in both paid and unpaid positions during the war years. Early in 1942, they were recruited along with men to be aircraft observers who learned to identify more than 50 types of aircraft in anticipation of an attack from the skies. Others were called to serve very long hours on the rationing board—a particularly thankless task. Still others went to Sacramento or the Bay Area to work in factories to support the war effort.

In 1944, A.L. Gilbert expanded operations with the purchase of this three-story building on North Yosemite Avenue and A Street, which originally served as the Tulloch family's Stanislaus Milling and Power Company. Gilbert's sons Bill, Bob, and Lawrence returned after wartime service to join the business. The men pictured are unidentified.

About 1928, A.L. Gilbert introduced Ladino Clover to the area. It proved an extraordinarily successful crop and profoundly changed the local agricultural economy. Providing permanent pasture on previously unirrigated land, it offered excellent forage for cattle, sheep, and turkeys. Two million lambs were reportedly fattened on the clover in fields around Oakdale in the 1930s. In 1950, the chamber of commerce proclaimed Oakdale "the Ladino Clover Center of America."

The Van Pelt company plane is shown next to one of their fire trucks in this photograph from 1950. George Chappell was an engineer in the plant as well as the company pilot. Chappell started as a janitor in 1937 and left to serve in the army as a combat engineer during World War II. He returned to Van Pelt and worked his way up to vice president and part owner of the company. (Courtesy of Lynn Chappell.)

Sid Haiden was a pilot during World War II and was discharged as a major before returning to his hometown of Oakdale. He owned and operated dump trucks before opening Haidlen Ford Sales at 500 East F Street in 1955. Haidlen, then age 33, was believed to be the youngest Ford dealer in the manufacturer's history at that time. In 1966, he moved the dealership to its present location.

The Oakdale area has been the setting for many Hollywood movies. At left, in *Bound for Glory*, David Carradine, portraying folk singer Woody Guthrie, walks along the Sierra Railroad tracks on the east side of Oakdale ready to jump a freight train and head out of town. The film won the Academy Award for Best Cinematography, and film critic Roger Ebert called it "one of the best looking films ever made."

Oakdale celebrated 50 years as an incorporated city in 1956 with a grand Golden Jubilee. Here, movie and TV star Thomas Mitchell (left) congratulates Mayor Bill Reynolds (center) and Vice Mayor Gene Bianchi. Reynolds arrived in Oakdale in 1913 and was the Southern Pacific station agent and telegrapher until he retired in 1949. He served as mayor from 1952 to 1958 and proposed the idea of the four-day Golden Jubilee celebration.

Five

MOVER AND SHAKERS

O.Z. Bailey's mule team pulls a large load down G Street. As well as hay and "anything not connected at both ends," he literally moved buildings all over town and eventually became the town's long-serving and much-admired fire chief. He represents the industrious and enterprising citizens who made early Oakdale a thriving community. Entrepreneurs and homemakers, rich and poor, prominent and humble—this chapter briefly tells some of their stories.

P.L. Huntley practices with his sisters (from left to right) Laura, Mattie, and Julia. Huntley was a contractor and talented musician who performed often at local events. He built several Oakdale churches, homes, and commercial buildings. The night he finished work on the *Oakdale Leader* office in 1895, the barn next door caught fire and burned part of the just-completed building. His wife's millinery shop on West Railroad Avenue also burned.

James Endicott and his brother Richard came to Oakdale in 1888 to practice medicine and surgery. By 1890, they had moved into the Odd Fellows Building and opened a drugstore. Dr. Endicott was a strong political partisan and a forceful debater who was "remarkably well informed on all matters pertaining to political history," according to the *Oakdale Leader*.

Gabriel "G.L." Rodden, born in North Carolina, made his way to Tuolumne County in the 1850s, where he initially engaged in freighting materials from Stockton to the Mother Lode mines. He moved with his family to Oakdale after the railroad arrived. They purchased large tracts of land, engaged in retail and commercial enterprises, and were heavily involved in civic activities, helping to shape the young community.

Brothers William (left) and Edward Rodden moved to Oakdale with their father, G.L. Rodden, in 1879. They opened a mercantile business and purchased real estate, becoming two of the largest land owners in the area. In 1893, Will Rodden narrowly escaped serious injury when the wheel of a wagon he was driving came off. He fell out and the frightened horse ran over him, knocking him unconscious.

Ada Drew Rodden met her future husband, Edward, when he delivered groceries from his family store to the Cottle residence, where she was living while attending school in Oakdale. They married in 1888. She and her sister-in-law Ada were active in several civic and social organizations. When their husbands donated land for a park and clubhouse in 1909, the Ladies Improvement Society proposed the name Dorada Park in their honor.

Lola, Eddie, Mellie, and Willie, seen here about 1900, were the children of Ada and Ed Rodden. Mellie was an accomplished pianist and star of the Oakdale Union High School girls' basketball team. She entered Stanford University in 1910. In 1905, her brother Willie was a student at the San Francisco Business College preparing to join the Rodden family's extensive banking, real estate, and cattle businesses.

In 1901, the *Oakdale Leader* proclaimed of William Rodden, "There is no more successful businessman in this town . . . he can do a whole lot of business in a short space of time . . . and does everything on the square." He and his brother Edward owned land just north of the Stanislaus River along what is now Rodden Road and successfully enticed many Italian farmers to the area.

Dora Woods married William Rodden in 1884. She had moved to Oakdale earlier that year with her parents, who owned and operated the White House Hotel. She was one of the founders of the Ladies Improvement Club, which continues today as the Oakdale Women's Club. During the influenza epidemic of 1918, Dora coordinated the effort to make 90 "pneumonia jackets" for patients at the Oakdale Hospital.

William "W.A." Griffin was born in Georgia in 1836. At age 25, he enlisted in the Confederate Army of Tennessee. He participated in many of the major battles of the Civil War and was promoted to first lieutenant for gallantry on the field of battle. In 1864, Griffin sustained a serious wound that crippled his arm for the rest of his life. He came to the Oakdale area in 1869.

A man of keen intellect and a student of public affairs, William Griffin was elected justice of the peace for Oakdale in 1894, and thereafter had the honorific title of "Judge" Griffin. He was editor and publisher of the *Oakdale Leader* from 1899 to 1909 and is shown here in the *Leader* office in 1906.

Jacob Haslacher (pictured) and his partner and brother-in-law Louis Kahn took Oakdale by storm when they moved to town to establish a general merchandise store in 1885. They soon became important grain merchants, building a series of large warehouses at various points along the railroad. They also engaged in land speculation, sometimes buying 1,000 acres or more at a time. They founded the Bank of Oakdale in 1888.

Fanny Haslacher was married to Jacob Haslacher. Her sister Celia was married to Louis Kahn. Fanny was a skilled gardener, famous for the beautiful roses she grew at her home on Second Avenue. She was active in supporting local schools and was a tireless fundraiser for the Masonic Orphans Home. (Courtesy of the Bank of Stockton.)

RES of LOUIS KAHN, F. ST. OAKDALE, CAL.

This is the Oakdale home of Louis Kahn and his wife, Celia Frankenheimer Kahn. He and his partner Jacob Haslacher sold everything from silk parasols to Studebaker wagons in their general merchandise store. Kahn was a member of the Masonic lodge and supported a number of civic activities, including the annual Firemen's Ball. Louis and Celia's daughter Rheta attended Mills College in Oakland.

Celia Kahn was married to Luis Kahn and was sister-in-law to Jacob Haslacher. She was appointed administratrix of her husband's estate after his death by a self-administered gunshot wound in 1905. She had a huge legal mess on her hands resulting from the failure of the Bank of Oakdale and was still trying to settle legal problems in the courts until her death in 1923.

Stella Schadlich appears to put little son Ray, holding a broom, to work in front of their home on the northeast corner of F Street and North Second Avenue. Stella and her husband, Henry, were lifelong residents of Oakdale and were involved in many commercial and civic activities. Roy graduated with honors from UC Berkeley in 1927 and joined a San Francisco accounting firm.

Peter and Emma Jorgensen stand on the porch of the home he built in 1902 in anticipation of their marriage. Jorgensen was a native of Denmark who had come to the United States at age 17 in 1885. He established the Oakdale Soda Works in 1896 was an active member of Oakdale's volunteer fire department, serving as chief from 1899 to 1901.

Chris Walther (second from left) came from Germany with his family to Oakdale at the age of four. He was a blacksmith and wheelwright with a shop on East Railroad Avenue, which is pictured here. He received regional recognition when he fabricated the body of Oakdale Union School's first school bus on a Chevrolet chassis in 1919.

Brothers James and Otis Ames came from Maine to Oakdale in about 1885 and married sisters. They were successful inventors of well-drilling equipment whose wives were "active assistants in their industrial pursuits," according to the newspaper. Their family Christmas picture shows them in front of a decorated orange tree. It became a postcard circulated throughout the country, advertising Oakdale's mild climate.

Eva Stearns (right) was a graduate of
Oakdale High School and a 1907 graduate
of the San Francisco Normal School. She
began teaching in Sonoma County but
moved back to teach elementary school
in Oakdale. She is pictured with her
younger sister Edna. In 1908, the *Oakdale
Leader* reported that Eva and Edna had
returned from a short trip to Sacramento
"where they had the time of their lives."

Anne Endicott, daughter of Anna and Elmer
Endicott and granddaughter of Dr. James
Endicott, graduated from Oakdale Union
High School in 1916. The *Oakdale Leader*
described her as "both pretty and charming
and popular among the younger set and
much beloved by the old-time residents for
her loyal nature and friendship." She married
Emmett Smith of Modesto in 1922.

In 1933, a Stockton radio station broadcast a program from the Almond Blossom Festival and featured a solo by Dorothy Coppetti, accompanied by the Oakdale High School orchestra. The following year, she was crowned queen by the "Spirit of Water," portrayed by Hazel Kaufman, in an elaborate ceremony. The *Modesto Bee* estimated that an amazing crowd of 30,000 people attended the two-day festival. (Courtesy of the Coppetti and Walther families.)

Arriving from Nebraska in 1910, Bert Holton decided he very much liked California weather. "There are only two kinds of weather here," he told the *Oakdale Leader*, "usual and unusual." He was recruited into the volunteer fire department soon after arriving in town. In this photograph, Holton holds the door open for the ladies who appear to be taking up all the seats, so the young man will be driving the family's horse. (Courtesy of Ken Terpstra.)

The A.L. Gilbert home was under construction by Frank Fowler in 1904. No other houses appear near the southwest corner of Second Avenue and A Street at that time. This house still stands on the site and has been described as a magnificent example of the Neoclassical Craftsman style. Fowler built houses in different styles for many of Oakdale's prominent citizens.

A.L. Gilbert is pictured here with his young son Lawrence in about 1911. He and his wife, Emma Banks Gilbert, had five children: four boys and one girl. Their young daughter Jeannette died of measles in 1913 at the age of six. The measles virus was a frequent cause of death and disability in the days before a vaccine was available, and affected rich and poor alike.

Tomasa Perez Griffith came to Oakdale in 1881 from Big Oak Flat, California. In 1905, she opened the locally famous Tamale House on East Railroad Avenue. "Mother Griffith" took in at least 44 children over the years, regardless of the ability of their parents (if known or even alive) to pay for their care. She also provided food and lodging for the town's elderly poor and served as an interpreter in the local court system. In 1942, she was featured as the Good Neighbor of the Day on the national radio broadcast of *Breakfast at Sardi's*. In nominating her for the honor, Evelyn Marshall wrote, "This lady has raised 40 children, not one being her own . . . but one and all, she gave them a mother's tender care just as she would, had they been her own. Many of them are now holding very responsible positions due mainly to her sacrifices for them. In addition to raising all these children, she somehow found time to extend a helping hand to others who were sick or in trouble."

Emmett Richardson (right) enlisted in the hospital corps soon after the United States entered World War I in 1917. He qualified for officer's training and achieved the rank of lieutenant. Velma Reeder (center) volunteered with the Women's Working Corps of the Red Cross chapter in Oakdale. She married Ben Yeager (left) in 1919.

After enlisting in the US Army in 1917, Oakdale resident Carl Muheim was sent to Camp Lewis in Washington. After recovering from measles, he was ordered to France with other young men from Oakdale. Despite being wounded in his thigh in the Battle of the Argonne, he continued to fight until a shrapnel wound rendered him unconscious. For weeks, his family at home did not know he had survived.

Dr. J. Audley Young (back row, far right) looks amused at the outlandish outfits some of his guests are wearing on the porch of his home on South Third Avenue. Soon after graduation from medical school, Dr. Young took over his father's practice in Oakdale. At the onset of World War I, he volunteered for service and was sent to France to join the 160th Field Hospital. While serving there, he wrote to his friend Ed Schadlich, asking to borrow a pair of field glasses until the end of the war. The government was very short of basic supplies. Field glasses were especially important since communications were sometimes confused, and officers needed as much visual confirmation of chaotic situations as they could possibly get. Dr. Young was discharged as a major at the end of the war and returned to his practice in Oakdale.

March Fong Eu was born in 1922 in her parents' Oakdale home. She graduated from UC Berkeley and then obtained an EdD from Stanford. She was elected to the California State Assembly in 1966, and secretary of state of California in 1974. She was not only the first woman to hold the office, but the first Asian American woman elected to a state office in the United States.

Harry Low (left) was born in Oakdale in 1931, where his parents operated the Hop Lee Laundry. He graduated from Oakdale Union High School, attended UC Berkeley Law School, and was the first Asian American to pass the bar in California. He became a highly respected jurist in San Francisco.

Kenneth Kaufman moved to Oakdale from Kansas as a child when his father, Sam, joined partners to establish the Pacific Pea Packing Company. Kenneth was a star basketball player at Oakdale Union High School and president of the student body when he graduated in 1913. He became manager of the cannery, and he, his brothers, and his father bought out their partners in 1936.

Jim and Pat Titchenal look like they could be strolling down Hollywood Boulevard rather than a street in their Oakdale hometown. The popular and attractive young couple were married soon after Jim returned from service during the Korean War. Jim, a talented musician, was active in the chamber of commerce and was elected president of the Oakdale Dinner Club. He was a distributor for the Standard Oil Company.

Eddie LeBaron, an All-American legend known as the "Little General," graduated from Oakdale High School at age 16. He played football at the College of the Pacific under famed coach Amos Alonzo Stagg. After recovering from wounds sustained during the Korean War, he played for the Washington Redskins. He was NFL Rookie of the Year in 1952 and participated in four Pro Bowls. In his off-seasons, he earned a law degree.

Visco Grgich, a native of Yugoslavia, was an offensive guard and a defensive tackle on the San Francisco 49ers' first team in 1946. A knee injury ended his pro-football career in 1952. In 1957, he was hired as head football coach for the Oakdale High School Mustangs. He worked and lived in Oakdale for the next 49 years.

The Oakdale Dinner Club, formed in November 1923, has met regularly for the last 100 years. In 1939, the *Oakdale Leader* declared, "no other single organization has contributed so much to the development of community cooperation." This picture from the early 1950s seems to confirm the club's original goal: "to foster a spirit of good fellowship and sociability," although why Mayor Bill Reynolds is handing out cash is a bit of a mystery. The club faced a challenge during World War II when rationing made it difficult for restaurants, caterers, and even citizens to get particular foods and ingredients. However, it persevered, and to this day continues to meet, have a good time, support worthwhile causes, and promote a spirit of community cooperation. From left to right are J.B. Pecchenino, Harold Blume, P.E. Van Pelt, Chester Baley, Mayor Reynolds, and George Chappell. (Courtesy of Lynn Chappell.)

Young Lynn Chappell (left) and friends surround police chief Clay Dorroh. The long-serving chief was especially admired for his work with Oakdale's youth and was awarded a lifetime membership in the PTA. He initiated Oakdale's annual Halloween parade. Even after 70 years, local children and adults still look forward to the parade and the refreshments each fall.

In 1956, this group participated in a tour of Beardsley Dam and Donnell Dam sponsored by the chamber of commerce. The projects were being completed as part of the huge Tri-Dam Project. A joint venture of the Oakdale Irrigation District and the South San Joaquin Irrigation District, the dams, along with Tulloch Dam, continue to provide water for irrigation of over 100,000 acres and hydroelectric power.

Born in Oakdale about 1878, Reyer "Riley" Kattestaart was a veteran of the Spanish-American War, a cowboy, a hunter, a teamster, and a popular storyteller. For many years, he sat on this fire hydrant on the northwest corner of F Street and Yosemite Avenue. Friends gifted him with a specially constructed cushion and a silver belt buckle with an image of the fireplug in gold.

This photograph of Florabel McKenzie Brennan promoted her slim pamphlet, *Along the Stanislaus 1806–1906*. It was published by the *Oakdale Leader* in 1956 to celebrate the town's Golden Jubilee. A 1909 graduate of Oakdale High School, Brennan attended the Western Normal School in Stockton briefly before passing California's teachers examination. By the fall of 1910, she was appointed principal of the Knights Ferry School. (Courtesy of the *Oakdale Leader*.)

Mrs Dan Brennan standing behind Antique Rocker presented to her Father from Sup't of Alta Mine in 1895.Knights Ferry Califormia.

124

Velma and Ben Yeager were crowned king and queen to reign over Oakdale's four-day Golden Jubilee celebration. Velma was a 1915 graduate of Oakdale Union High School. After completing a course at Heald's Business College in Stockton, she went to work for the Pacific Pea Packing Company. There, she met Ben Yeager, and the couple were married in 1919.

Pictured from left to right are Shirley Cheek, Gene Bianchi, Harold Walther, and Leonard Krause. Everyone with a horse was invited to saddle up and ride in the big parade celebrating Oakdale's Golden Jubilee in 1956. Cheek, manager of the chamber of commerce; Bianchi, city councilman and chairman of the event; and Walther, city councilman, rode in a vintage stagecoach. Krause, Saddle Club president, rode his horse along with hundreds of other cowboys and cowgirls.

Hall of Fame cowboy Harley May and his bronc take a hard fall during the Oakdale Rodeo. The Oakdale Saddle Club was formed in 1945 and quickly grew to over 100 members. The club purchased 20 acres east of Oakdale and organized its first annual Clover Roundup in 1946. It was attended by more than 4,500 people. In 1954, the Saddle Club sponsored its first annual professional rodeo and continued calling it the Clover Roundup until the name was officially changed to the Oakdale Rodeo in 1957. Local cowboys like John Bowman—and later, Harley May, Jim Charles, Ace Berry, the Camarillo brothers, and others—won national awards and helped establish the town as "the Cowboy Capitol of the World." The Oakdale Rodeo continues to be a popular event, and each year, the club awards the John Bowman memorial trophy to the best all-around cowboy.

Betty Saletta's life-size bronze sculpture of a horse and rider—*Yesterday is Tomorrow*—can be seen alongside F Street in front of the Cowboy Museum. It sits appropriately near the old Southern Pacific train depot, which was at the center of early Oakdale life. This impressive work celebrates the town's Western heritage and its continuing influence on our community. In this small volume, only some of the people and events from Oakdale's past could be introduced. There is so much more to know, so please continue to explore, learn, and contribute to the understanding of Oakdale's history. (Photograph by Don Riise.)

DISCOVER THOUSANDS OF LOCAL HISTORY BOOKS
FEATURING MILLIONS OF VINTAGE IMAGES

Arcadia Publishing, the leading local history publisher in the United States, is committed to making history accessible and meaningful through publishing books that celebrate and preserve the heritage of America's people and places.

Find more books like this at
www.arcadiapublishing.com

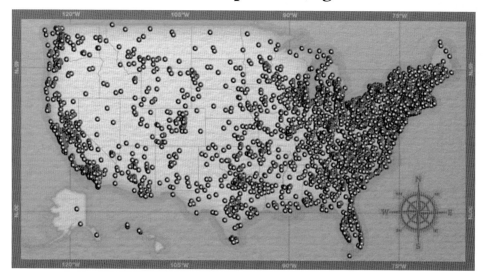

Search for your hometown history, your old stomping grounds, and even your favorite sports team.

Consistent with our mission to preserve history on a local level, this book was printed in South Carolina on American-made paper and manufactured entirely in the United States. Products carrying the accredited Forest Stewardship Council (FSC) label are printed on 100 percent FSC-certified paper.

MADE IN THE